PRIMERS

Volume Five

PRIMERS

Volume Five

Krystelle Bamford
Claire Cox
Hannah Jane Walker

Nine
Arches
Press

Primers: Volume Five
Krystelle Bamford, Claire Cox and Hannah Jane Walker
Selected by: Jacqueline Saphra and Jane Commane

ISBN: 978-1-911027-95-9
eBook ISBN: 978-1-911027-96-6

Copyright © Krystelle Bamford, Claire Cox and Hannah Jane Walker.

Cover image: © Jason Leung via Unsplash

All rights reserved. No part of this work may be reproduced, stored or transmitted in any form or by any means, graphic, electronic, recorded or mechanical, without the prior written permission of the publisher.

The individual authors have asserted their rights under Section 77 of the Copyright, Designs and Patents Act 1988 to be identified as the authors of this work.

First published July 2020 by:

Nine Arches Press
Unit 14, Sir Frank Whittle Business Centre,
Great Central Way, Rugby.
CV21 3XH
United Kingdom

www.ninearchespress.com

Nine Arches Press is supported using public funding by Arts Council England.

About the Selecting Editors:

Jacqueline Saphra is a poet and playwright. Her first collection, *The Kitchen of Lovely Contraptions* (flipped eye, 2011) was shortlisted for the Aldeburgh First Collection Prize. *If I Lay on my Back I Saw Nothing but Naked Women* (The Emma Press, 2017) won The Saboteur Award for Best Collaborative Work. In 2017, *A Bargain with the Light: Poems after Lee Miller* was published by Hercules Editions and her collection from Nine Arches Press, *All My Mad Mothers*, was shortlisted for the 2017 T.S. Eliot prize. Her most recent play, *The Noises,* funded by the T.S. Eliot Foundation and Arts Council England, was produced at The Old Red Lion Theatre in 2019. Jacqueline's collection, *Dad, Remember You are Dead* (Nine Arches Press) was also published in 2019 and followed by *Veritas: Poems after Artemisia* (Hercules Editions) in April 2020, a chapbook of sonnets celebrating Artemisia Gentileschi, the greatest woman painter of the late Italian Renaissance. Jacqueline lives in London and teaches at The Poetry School. www.jacquelinesaphra.com

Jane Commane is a poet, editor and publisher. Her first full-length collection, *Assembly Lines,* was published by Bloodaxe in 2018. A graduate of the Warwick Writing Programme, for a decade she also worked in museums and archives and in 2016 she was chosen to join Writing West Midlands' Room 204 writer development programme. Jane is editor at Nine Arches Press, co-editor of *Under the Radar* magazine, and is co-author, with Jo Bell, of *How to Be a Poet,* a creative writing handbook (Nine Arches Press). In 2017, she was awarded a Jerwood Compton Poetry Fellowship. In 2019, Jane was commissioned by Historic England and the Poetry Society for the *Where Light Falls* project to write a poem alongside community groups which was projected as part of a music, poetry and light installation onto the ruins of Coventry Cathedral and viewed by over 15,000 people over three nights.

Contents

Foreword	9

Krystelle Bamford

Epiphany, Age Three	13
Rites	14
1-Up: Elegy for the Year 2000	15
Still Life with Janitor	16
At the Great Forest's Edge	17
Animism	18
O	19
To All the Girls, Mid-Air	20
Wake	21
Middle Life	22
On Describing *The Shining* to Someone Who's Never Seen It	23
Two Lies: the deer	24
Dad	26
Upon Seeing at the National Gallery the Largest Extant Pieter Saenredam Painting with My Baby	27
Catch You on the Flip Side	28
E.T.	29

Claire Cox

After Dark	33
My Brother as a Sentimentalist	34
Parlour Games	35
Thicker than Water	36
My Brother as a Mezzotint	37
Hospital Sandwiches	38
Treatment	39
Entity	40
Windsucker	41

Slow Release	42
Cortège	43
Funeral	44
My Brother as an Astronaut	45
My Brother as a Shoebox	46
Unremembering	47
How to Mend a Brother	48

Hannah Jane Walker

A study at 20	51
Spread like milk across his bed	52
No one knows where you are	53
The shark experience	54
The most 90s poem ever	55
Pageant	56
Miscarriage	57
Palmistry	58
The woman who made my engagement bracelet	59
Trying not to have a Big Day	60
Through five filters	61
Untellable	62
The sex we have	64
Induction	65
My mother's aria	66
I love you so much that I want to explain	67

Acknowledgements   69

FOREWORD

The Primers poetry mentoring scheme began in 2015 with the intention of finding and supporting exciting poetry by a range of debut poets. Primers has now published sixteen new poets, with each selected by a guest judge and receiving one-to-one mentoring and editing advice, all designed to take their poetry into print and out into the world.

The 2019 call for submissions brought us a rich variety of new writing. In reading through these submissions, we witnessed many new poets finding their wings; soaring into experiments and daring ideas, or distinctive voices discovering their own ways of being heard, of honing the world into words.

The work you will read here stood out early on in the selection process as creating a lived experience for the reader on the page. Each of these poets moved us from a very first read with courage, openness and authenticity and each walks an exhilarating edge, daring to take risks with both language and content.

Krystelle Bamford's poems take on two of poetry's universal themes with the airiest of touches, a dextrous use of white space and some extraordinary imagery: birth and death co-exist in this selection and it is the juxtaposition of these two life experiences - of becoming a mother and losing a father - that leaves the reader enlightened and changed.

Claire Cox digs deep into love and grief and carries us along in the tide of feelings associated with loss. The relationship between brother and sister is held implacably in the light. This narrative of death and dying, negotiating childhood, cancer treatment and loss universalises the personal with a courageous and intimate directness.

Hannah Jane Walker, with her frank and disarming tales of coming-of-age, creates a visceral and immediate world and invites us in. The call is irresistible. We travel with her through tales of twenty-something sex and eventual self-actualisation that gives way to observations on love, marriage and motherhood expressed with imaginative dexterity, humour and pathos.

It was a great pleasure and learning experience to share discussion of these poems with each other in the selection process. The job of the mentor, as we see it, is in supporting the poet to make their poem into the artefact it is yearning to be. This involves close listening to both the poem and poet and careful consideration of the synergy of form and content. It means preserving the best spontaneous elements whilst tightening and strengthening the frames of the poems. It means honouring the vulnerability and delicacy of the work. The mentoring process is a three-way dialogue between the mentor, the poet and poem where the poem must always have the last word. All three poets were open to change and experimentation and worked with a deep commitment. We are honoured to be a part of their journey and very proud of this book.

Our thanks and admiration also to the other six poets shortlisted, Juliet Antill, Kathryn Bevis, Claire Collison, Eve Ellis, Thyrza Leyshon and Ian Walker, whose striking and multifarious work we also much appreciated – we hope that a Primers shortlisting has been an encouraging recognition for you and your poems, and we extend our gratitude to the longlisted poets whose poetry also caught our eye.

2020 may not be the easiest time in which to be first published as a poet, but though the world around us is uncertain, anxious and strange, poetry itself feels only ever more vital. In its writing, poetry can allow us to comprehend, contain and express what has been encountered and experienced; in its reading, poetry's innate ability to make a fellowship that bridges both commonalities and differences through a deep and vital connection in language. The poems from Krystelle Bamford, Claire Cox and Hannah Jane Walker, published here in *Primers: Volume Five*, uniquely create for their readers an illuminating, attentive space in which to share something seen, heard, and understood together.

Jacqueline Saphra and Jane Commane,
July 2020.

Krystelle Bamford

Krystelle Bamford's poetry has appeared in *The American Poetry Review*, *The Kenyon Review*, *Under the Radar*, *The Scores* and a number of anthologies. She received a Scottish Book Trust New Writers Award, was shortlisted for the Bridport Prize and longlisted for the 2019 National Poetry Competition. Raised in the US, she now lives in Scotland where she worked at Canongate Books, completed a Creative Writing MLitt at the University of St Andrews and gave birth to two wee, radge kids.

Epiphany, Age Three

I miss your apple-bright pelt my loaf, my oat,
my snow-drowsed companion – little face at the leaded glass,
under the fir and all the brittle fruit you'd hung the night before.
It's those three magisterials of Orientzar,
weary, heavy with scent, swaying across starfields on reindeer,
stepping from out the Dead Sea –
you await them, their gifts, in the still of the night
in the boughs of your tree.
And then the brilliance of morning
and then years and more years and then me.

Rites

A canoe cuts towards Plum Island Sound, silver, stem high.
Morning makes its incision along the ridge of deciduous and
      evergreen trees.
I have loved you all my life; it was you who first explained
the headhunters of Borneo, trailed by their prizes, ash-lidded, shtum
smaller-than-life. You held a pipe in your teeth as you drove with
      the dog in your lap
then died in your bed (you, who once said you'd like to end like a Viking
at sea with the beast at your feet). We've walked back
the last book to the library, taken your name off the bills. Still –
your tobacco sleeps near the remote, lightly as tinder; the dog
at the door. Waves of black water, fire.

1-Up: Elegy for the Year 2000

This is all before the plane hit and the plane hit
again. I courted danger then. I loved it
like a girl loves a horse. I stroked its long nose.

Would you rather sink with a leaden face
or dance atop a flagpole at your end? I did it both ways –
I ground down or burned then burst

from that hole with seeds in my teeth
brazen as spring. Now it's all goombas
all day, a parliament of pale, nipping heads,

Bob-omb, then nothing. But also? A daughter's birth,
the long blood of it, the hard summoning
from some monster-free realm where wrack

is unknown fruit: my golden coin
my gleaming girl
whatever is the opposite of ruin.

Still Life with Janitor
Gordon College Physical Plant, Wenham MA

God he loved to read. He was a seed, the staked ash sapling
then ash tree. He waxed their floors, held their keys, consumed
    their library:
under the resin of greenglass lamps he lived entirely.
And all that time a growth in him, the CAT scan's livid weed.
As he grew it grew too, scalloped, knotted, dimming. And all
    that time
he wiped their boards he taught me everything. *Sing it.*
And all that time I answered friends 'Oh Dad?
He's faculty.' *Do it.* Dad as cash-lean junkie. *Sing it.*
Dad as cowled apothecary. *Do it.*
And all that time this thing right here
laced its roots through me – *do it*:
        back bent like a spoon to a flame my dad over a froth
            of bills my dad until he dissolved
                into this my dad
                      whatever's left
                              from the graft my dad
    may it spring from the edges   and bloom my dad
                let it turn its green face to the moon

At the Great Forest's Edge

Away from the vegetal sleepers sleeping
bed pans   warmed bricks   mothers
and their milktoothed fateful gears
to where the trees begin   like a baby
it calls and you've come
no coat   no shoes   newly named   *Snipped String*   *Vanished Crumb*
no more moths   bent pennies   starch
or make-do for you   *Chicken Bone*   *Sweet Treat*
only boughs strung up in endless arcades   black hardened sugar
and snow
         no matter   *Son-of-Mine*   *No-Son-of-Mine*
         that your mother is cradling her head with worry
         on a kitchen table once bigger than the world
         to you   *Spotted Thief*   *Lost Shoe*
curse the industry and too-small mercies of mothers
what waits for you   wants you
Littlest Joint   *Drop-of-Blood*
ancient in its christening dress
Echo-in-the-Well-of-Me
Chit-of-All-My-Days
patiently
         and all desire

Animism

When my dog sneezes I bless her and hope she understands
that I'm sorry for shouting, that we're all very lost in this house.

I have no way of saying he won't arrive any minute,
brown paper bags heavy with cheese and sardines

to feed her from the table what he himself ate
as if to say you are me, only smaller.

Of late I have learned to keen like an animal and because I am not,
to wonder at the quality of my keening – ragged and strange

and altering. Crying like death is ugly so here then, make me ugly
like a slavering beast, make me whole like a faultless beast,

and we can howl and root and piss on the night roses
and that will serve as our blessing.

O

the heart is still a wire
an undersea fibre optic
and everything is warmed
now by this little wire

my bones speak to each other
now that I am older   they twitter
roosted in their sockets
across my forest floor

we dialed O we dialed
with our fingers then our voices
it doesn't really fucking matter
he's not there O he's not there

To All the Girls, Mid-Air

I was stupid too: a shy lace curtain, leather tool
an empty basin caned with white, and me a bride-to-be.
I really loved the bad ones – we all do!
Though we change ourselves in flight   little Leda's budding pinions
oof the neb, the gaping end of that trajectory.
If I could touch the down behind your ear
I'd lean right in and murmur *stay*   up there, the apogee
                                      tray unfolded, belt undone
in the placid filtered grey strung between the grit and sun.

Wake

for my grandpa, Françis Royer

Some go in violets.
      Others through the screen door.
Some have something
      in the pocket – say,
            a racing slip
            if they loved
            the greyhounds
            best.

Will you travel by boat?
      What will you think
            when the water won't wet
            your cuffs, when you find
            your fear
                  of water is gone?

Some go in cock's comb,
      bleeding heart,
      forget-me-not.
      It doesn't matter. Go
            incognito
            for once in your life.
            I'll cup your head
      if someone
takes your heels.

Middle Life

There are many kinds of hearts.
That of T. Rex might have been the exact
size of you, right now. We'll never know.
All their hearts have gone off and left us only their houses
just like in *Citizen Kane*.
To say if those stooped, careering despots
ever loved anything at all we'd first need to sift their bones
and read them like dregs of the hot mug you're cradling now
in the fleeting hours before work, before
the final asteroidal blast as you graze   a half-step
from grace, through the epochs and strata of middle life
with all the lushness and terror that implies.

On Describing *The Shining* to Someone Who's Never Seen It

The father, is he sad? I don't know. He's happy
at the end, flattens into the wallpaper, parquet,
grows spiny and dark like the hedges.

Some people die, yes; some come already dead.
In this place even the innocents are terrifying, blank
as an egg. The house is too still, under its shell. Yes,

he was probably sad but we never see it. No
lesson to learn except maybe that some of us shine
and some of us don't. Or maybe there's something

in the survivors stumbling out into new snow,
blinking, bewildered, like it was his last
most beautiful gift.

Two Lies: the deer

creep as only deer can
they don't consider it creeping though –
we parade on their backs
high gloss   patina-on-death
like palanquins for heartbreak
but I suspect their hearts hold only
tubers sinew bone and teeth

        on the last day
        you didn't know me anymore
        from under the morphine's heavy brocade

so the deer (unmoved) move   are moved
through patterns of light and sound
by some deer-shaped force within;
or they're still as the character for deer
always bending its fine head
to the ground forever

        or maybe
        you knew but couldn't say
        mixing as you were
        with light and sound
        your words moving away

no the deer in lacquered heels creep
crowned in grief through bracken halls
they creep towards us
under dimmet's low eaves
embroidered with sorrow
they're creeping for us

and yes
it's me hold me close
hold me higher still
I'm coming I'm home
I'll see you soon

Dad
after Sylvia Plath

I can't make it beautiful
and true. You're now a candle,
unlit, among the batteries,
loose change, calcified glue

or the Mary Celeste
when a light skiff would do.

The internet's glistering pulse
has nothing on you. I search for a blessing
to a phantom atchoo.

I'll wait for my life –
you're every- and nowhere
more shade than hue

both gone as they come
and long overdue.

Upon Seeing at the National Gallery the Largest Extant Pieter Saenredam Painting with My Baby

The biggest and the utter smallest, they call out to each other,
two golden constructions twinned in the darkest coil
of their beginning. Everything is always

calling out to her, god help us. These old Dutch churches
were gilded and marbled but the church in the painting
is clean in itself like a tree is clean in itself, or a baby.

Colonnades grow and touch then retreat from us
marvelling. My daughter, now strapped to my chest
will leave me one day, the brat;

I'm the scaffolding that comes away.
Yet here (*she reaches*) breezing in from the canvas's edge
the supplicants – black hatted, honeyed

for her, yes, as it should be.

Catch You on the Flip Side
August 6, 2012

There is a beginning, middle and there is an end, dragging around sheaves of black crepe, setting accidental fires, eating uncleanly from the hors d'oeuvres. My end might look like this: your giant, tear-slicked nose lowering itself from a rafter bristling with angels. Your end looked like this: me switching off the light.

The beginning is what? I was wrapped around the tree of the world, a little hand around a bigger hand. I was standing on the back of myself. I was my own daughter though lesser of course as my daughter repels all invaders, painted, furred, and otherwise.

The middle is the seagulls born each year all over our roof. It's sweating through winter armour and calling through tunnels of snow. It's the string that holds one mitten to the other, preventing loss at all cost. Before you go, tell me again –

what was it that we'd wanted all this time? My end might look like this:
        a) everything I ever hoped for
        b) a long black rest
        c) you, finally,
                switching on the light

E.T.

Marianne, when you were born you were so beautiful
I thought you would kill me – a doorless craft on the forest floor.
Festooned in guts, painted all over in my own DNA, you fooled no one,
so obviously beyond my making. I was dying to ask
all the usual questions: *Where did you come from? Who sent you?*
To call in the shadowy experts and let them take you away
to care for you, expertly. You were so beautiful
I was sure they would want you, who wouldn't
     Marianne?
Now you say *bagpipes, spiderweb, superman, please* as if this broken,
reeling place were your own, fluent in the borrowed language
of oxygen and heartache, practising faces in the mirror, the tradecraft
that will let you live among; let you leave again.

Claire Cox

Photograph credit: Gunilla Treen

Born in Hong Kong, **Claire Cox** now lives and works in Oxfordshire. She completed an M.A. in Creative Writing from Oxford Brookes University, winning the Blackwell's Prize for best student. Claire is Associate Editor for **ignition**press poetry pamphlet publishers, and is a part-time practice-based PhD student at Royal Holloway, University of London, studying poetry and disaster. Her poems have appeared in *Ink, Sweat & Tears, Magma, Envoi, Butcher's Dog* and *Lighthouse*.

After Dark

It's the time you call
black dog when late-night TV

hurls ghosts at the ceiling.
A man without time without

morphine you scrawl, your ink
as trip-wire as counter-hex

as anything that might keep out
the snap of its mantrap teeth.

My Brother as a Sentimentalist

You're chattering
in the passenger seat

bare hedgerows speed by
snagged with sunlight

vapour trails clutter
the winter-blue sky.

*There was a time
I didn't like them* you say

*But changed my mind
after Annie died*

*especially the ones
that cross – pretended*

*it was her
sending me kisses.*

I move our conversation on
you pull a smile I can't unpack.

Parlour Games

a basin of flour upturned
a coin dropped on its dusty pale dome

a bone-handled knife
passed sister to sister to brother

to mother to father
some shaved off the slightest puff

but you a boy
jostling towards manhood

cut closest of us all
tempting the forfeit

eager to pick out
the tumbled coin

with your teeth
then throwing back your head

nose lips chin
gauzy with flour

a sixpence to silver
your ghostly grin

Thicker than Water

In the clamour of a South Bank restaurant
you fixed a kiss to my cheek, called for drinks,
face too flushed, enthusiasm awry.
You talked and talked, saddened yourself
to stillness. Pulsed by the hurt I heard in your veins
I took your part as only blood can.
And while we puzzled the future
I watched you trace outlines: bare branches
on embankment trees, a light-caught curve,
the contours shaping a stranger's skin –
your artist's eye too tireless, too keen.

My Brother as a Mezzotint

Eager to admire your scans' monochrome tones
you lean forward in your wheelchair
study the luminous screen:
eclipsing your spinal cord, two dark moons;
the titanium caging your neck, pure black;
grey meat spills from your iliac's white wing.
The locum's chest is slim, boy-like,
his tired eyes rimmed by glasses
and concern, he answers our questions
with open hands. Not your own oncologist
he's unsure why his prognosis seems new.
Returning down the corridor you say *I'm glad*
it was you who was with me, reach across
to flatter an old woman on her tiger-stripe throw
as we pass wheel to wheel, then you charm
from the receptionist, so young and so plump,
the secret of her hidden tattoo.

Hospital Sandwiches

One bite and your name is called.
We flap, try to hide the scran

Must smarten up you hiss;
tuck in your shirt,

check your cap is straight, blush
like a schoolboy

summoned to see Headmaster
before I wheel you through.

Treatment

We'll only scan your dorsal spine today. Bleep 206 for the MacMillan Nurse. It's the spine causing your symptoms. Take slow release morphine   top up with Oramorph   to help with the pain. Bleep 206.   Siobhan will wheel you   from cubicle to   scanner. There'll be a chair.   Monica will do the CT scan today.   We'll tattoo   your front, not your   back.   Bleep   cubicle 206.   L2 and L3 are more involved with the   disease.   In the slow release   short term   we'll sequence   three areas for treatment. The side effects will be the same: vomiting and diarrhoea.   In the short term   Oramorph   top up   with the pain.   It's urgent.   Palliative.   In the short term   a doctor will look at the data   decide.   Side effects.   Vomiting.   Palliative. Cubicle.   Urgent.   We can only scan your dorsal spine today.

Entity

Lumped deep beneath the dene
under thick-leaved laurels

two paces beyond your bungalow wall
broken stones, rats and blackness:

the old ice house, its ruins
like a tumor in the earth.

Something rises from it
masses behind your bedstead

its breath scares you awake.
I help hang a talisman –

two lizards, each with the other's tail
between its teeth, a circle of bronze

unbroken you cast from
our mother's Chinese vase years ago.

We both know there's magic
in creation, we both hope

your makeshift ouroboros
will be potent enough

to lull the dark hunger
calm the bone-sucking chill.

Soon your wife will return
from her sister's. *Don't tell her*

you shush from your wheelchair
She'll not understand.

Windsucker

You, stabled in bed, pelvis cracked, knacker's yard thighs splayed
against steel rails; your blotched and skewbald skin.
You, tugging an over-washed hospital gown that slips
from your shoulders like some flimsy turnout rug.
The clack in your throat that kicks to a bray – again and again.

The nurses gauge your dosage in horsepower.
He's already had enough for ten they say,
not seeing the eleven wild mustangs that buck in your blood
thrashing to escape your burning bones.

Slow Release

You're a small boy in the time before
I was born, playing outside until dusk
steals all colour from your toy truck;
that time mum would have called *dimpsy*
shortens the garden to a rustling backdrop.

She's at the kitchen door, calling, getting cross.
In some secret den you turn your back
huddle tight over the treasures you've found that day.
Stubborn love has glued you to the dark, playing,
inventing a time outside of time.

And I have to know – as tears cauterise my eyes
and I stride down this hospital corridor
not to anything, simply away from your bedside –
why you won't just follow your body,
already releasing its thin cold scent of skin
atomising to dust,

why it is you're still here playing,
playing when all's dark
and someone is calling you home.

Cortège

They choose a wicker coffin.
On it, ferns plume wild
like a mislocated forest floor.

Your nephew and elder sister
step up with shrunken spines
shoulder your weight.

I walk behind, match their slow
march, watch one woven handle, step
by step, rub a pall-bearer's ear to blood.

Funeral

No order of service. Just a card
with your name, curlicued and slant,
year of birth, hyphen, year of death.
Above that, an old test print of yours
quizzing depth of cut, blackness,
how acid bites, how resin resists.
'Figure A' points to pale ripples:
a thumbprint in negative,
dabbed there momentarily –
your brief experiment in flesh.

My Brother as an Astronaut

lift-off
leaves behind ashes

in winter
in the distance between
frost and pulse

eye and space

a body lost
in morphine orbit

comes down

opens the casket
finds itself
gone

My Brother as a Shoebox

The sister-in-law's shed her funeral black
for a billowing tee-shirt, her silver plimsolls
squeeze past – *I've something for you* –
past the KEEP OUT! sign, sellotaped to a stool.
Floating on wine and anger I follow,
feel this new taboo slice my hip like wire.
I walk towards your room
whose mould I had scrubbed,
weighty bed shifted, floor cleared
where you'd spun your borrowed wheelchair.

She's searching, doubled over,
knee-deep in bin-bags.
Chairs, bed, our father's chest of drawers,
all vague contours beneath a plastic slick.
She sees me seeing. Pushes past
carrying something in her hands.
By the time I return to the sitting room,
fish bone, fur – all things indigestible –
she's dumped the cardboard box on the table
like a gull heaves a pellet.

Unremembering

If you answer this riddle,
You'll never begin.
– The Incredible String Band

Shake the mesh, let wire decide
what drops and what's kept.

Sift the clinker of your broken pelvis
the pebbled phlegm that knocked your throat.

Save only the wonderments you found in each day:
the suppleness of dubbin on walking-boot leather

the glaze that hides pink deep in its sheen
the folk tune resting in the hollow of your flute.

How to Mend a Brother

Take the door of his mouth, hammer it
shut. Roll up his tongue like a kilim rug.
Splice oak to his dry rot bones. Don't
inhale. Wear rubber gloves. Never sleep.

Get busy with a blowtorch. Ease
the black mould from every cell wall.
Scrub clean with sugar soap. Rinse.
Repair the crushed vaults of his lungs,
roller both rooms with oxygen and gloss.
Rewire his attic's strip light, its buzz
and flicker. Find the fusebox. Empty it
of Xanax. Make good. Then, before dusk

switch on each lamp, stand at the window –
keep watch, keep watch, keep watch

Hannah Jane Walker

Hannah Jane Walker is a writer from Essex. She makes work that uses poetry as a way of talking, in theatres, public spaces and for radio, working with BBC Radio 4, the British Council, and Apples and Snakes. With collaborator Chris Thorpe, she has created interactive shows exploring questions which seem too simple to ask, winning a Fringe First and touring the world. Plays are published by Oberon and performance poetry by Nasty Little Press. Poems in anthologies by Forest Fringe and Penned in the Margins. She often works with vulnerable groups, collaborating to create artworks. She is an Associate Artist for Cambridge Junction and National Centre for Writing.

A study at 20

Frankly, there is a lot I don't even admit to myself.
When I was in my twenties
I got really bloody-minded about asserting
my right to fuck whoever I wanted.
And apparently a lot of people wanted to fuck me.
I did things I can't quite face.
But I do it to myself sometimes, reveal the truth
in little squares.

Some of the sex was excellent.
Most of it was boring and required cleaning up.
Once I slept with a man whose girlfriend
was asleep in the next room.
It ended up feeling like a job.
I betrayed friends, replaced them with louder, camper
friends who brought me pastries and *Vogue* in bed.

I used plates as ashtrays,
took things that didn't belong to me,
took things I didn't know the name of
in the non-places, that become places
that made me feel I could see inside myself.

Spread like milk across his bed

I bet you were devastating when you were seventeen
I love a girl with a snaggletooth
I'd hate to be attractive wouldn't you?

He combs the Covent Garden cafes,
pockets filled with pens and postcards looking for girls
    whose poems feature
the colour of their hearts, their favourite moment of sky.

He feeds them cream cakes and tap water tepid as saliva.
Spread like milk across his bed he follows logic
    from shoulder to neck to ear.
Do you like your body?
Have you ever truly been loved?

When was the last time you gripped
a table, asked the whole room
to be quiet?

No one knows where you are

You drive me to a strip of neon,
buy beer and fried dumplings:
careful with the steam in your mouth.
You pull up in a place with no light.
You hold my wrist as we edge through the long grass.
What about snakes?
It's not them you need to be frightened of.
Tip your neck back.
The trees laden with colonies of fat coat hangers,
bats twitching in their sleep.

I will definitely die soon
and deserve it.
I brace.
We walk to a clearing.
This is why we came.

I wait for the blade between my ribs.
You gesture to the line of eucalyptus
and sigh, *usually girls love this.*

The shark experience

When she is ready, hair capped,
someone leads her lightly by the elbow,
past great pools of turquoise.

The rubber locker band grips her wrist –
the goggles fumbled, she
eclipses the ladder as her ankles dip.

The fin shudders the air grate –
blindly nose cuts the surface,
flank bumping bubbles off the tiles.

She lets the lights track her backstroke.
Her arms turnstile,
her sinuses inhale antiseptic.

They drop the meat in on string.
The red blue sinews wave in the water
then sink.

She sculls.
The hinge of her right knee crooks
then straightens.

It hangs steady circuits
browsing grouting
gills clogged air conditioning units.

Its eye, a still silver slit.

The most 90s poem ever

It's too hot on the patio. The T-shirt label scratches the back of her neck as she strips off in front of Helen's brother eating ketchup on toast. She slams her back flat on the paving slabs stares bare breasted at the flight path static. The old Labrador squats to do a shit. The eldest brother leans out the parents' window to squirt it with the Super Soaker.

The sun is anaesthetic. In great sleep swabs, she dreams of limes rolling off kitchen counters, swimming pools with open grates. Stepping shoeless through the garage door, her eyes adjust to the heft of the freezers. She helps herself to a Twister and a box of McCain chips.

In the kitchen the microwave is on an hour cycle cooking supper. Helen sits on the wood counter edge in hot-pants, she lifts up a banana with her foot.

In the brothers' room, Pamela Anderson and empty Lynx. She lets them chase her with the Super Soaker around the sun loungers and into the sitting room to drip on the carpet by the fake fireplace.

In the bathroom she stares out the framed Magic Eye picture while she shaves her bikini line with the elder brother's razor.

Pageant

When we run the pageant the teenagers get tipsy
dare each other to go shoulder deep
and wait for the fins

The sharks round here only come on certain types of days
Shark Days we call them
days when the cloud is low and the water dead
they like that
it lures them to the shoreline
A girl in a black bikini kneels on her catch
one hand on its neck
the other waving to the press

Miscarriage

The nice lady in sturdy shoes standing on the buttercup yellow floor
says catch it all in this cardboard bowl
we need to see it all.
I catch dove grey marble and red velvet
tip it into a specimen jar
hold it to the light – a seahorse bob.

I give it to her
and walk back down the hall
smiling at ladies in labour.

I feel the door of me shut
like in old films when the enemy arrives
a wooden bar thrown across a gate.

Palmistry

I see you are a wife and carry babies
like whitebait in a napkin.
Your friends never see you weeping.
I see you have a great fridge freezer
packed with mincemeat
and ice cubes.
Your daughter leans
on the kitchen island to ask
if you love her father.
Am I close?

Your downstairs toilet book selection is broad.
Your sateen sofa cushions, a triumph.

The woman who made my engagement bracelet

You know the way a landscape is –
silver twisted into strings by ice floats
glass nub softened by the dull beak of tides.

You know, when a field is turned over
and flint rolls itself out
of earth clods.

You know when the sea peels back
and the sand filters out
running away from itself.

You know, foot prints on rock.
Here you headed somewhere, here you danced a little, here
you fell to your hands like a dog.

You know, the sudden throw down
the crack and hiss of the geyser –
the bones of it.

In her workshop with only one wall
she tightens the clamp wrench
click twists on the butane ring,

anneals to berry red.
She grips the tongs, twists in rivers,
leans in to seal the circle.

Trying not to have a Big Day

The trunk is carried down from the attic,
the dress beaten and hung out to bleach.

After the truck-dust clears
100 white plastic chairs are unstacked into a grin.

The ceremony spot is tagged in black gaffer tape,
out of Zip-Lock primrose, marigold, geranium.

The kitchen drain runs blood and onions.
A small fridge for cold drinks cabled from the balcony.

Rocks are washed to weigh down the napkins.
White paper garlands shimmer building to building.

The USB backup in a labelled envelope
sellotaped to the underside of a speaker.

The stage is swept.
She washes her hair, plaits it, bracelets slip to her wrists:

To him she says, *it's just us
let's go get on with it.*

Through five filters

[Plain spoken]
We walked down to the sea
because we had given up hope
that we would have a child.

[lyric]
This walk was say goodbye
to the idea,
this tapering
un-talked thing.

[Cosmopolitan]
And when we got down to the water,
which is like quite far, as the tide goes miles
and the sand is so beautiful and so different
in every patch, I almost certainly said

[Technical]
*if we ever do have a child and it is a girl
let's call her Thea because it is the name
of the unknown planet that collided with earth
and produced the conditions for life,*

[Colloquial]
and your Dad laughed and said
you dickhead and kissed me.

Untellable

The only thing I can tell you is that birth is like surfing, she said.

Quickly learn the parameter of the board edge
force your bones up
tip forward
hunt distance
go again
and again
again
empty out content
ignore things that brush your limbs
all is surface.
Who knows how much water you hang over
you will pass what you knew of pain
learn to stop thought
forget language.
The leash attached to your ankle will vanish
when you are inhaling water
scrabbling to exit.
All is tide,
continent shifts
a street you lived
your mother's kneecap
a piece of pearl at the bottom of a green plastic bucket.
How far down the beach your belongings will seem,
things that belong to a stranger now, you'll think.
Allow it to slam your skull
don't tense resist
the current will rip apart your hips
lean in use your feet arches for leverage
push around the rock

offer the soft of your wrists
the blank of your neck
lichen
urchin
seal
basking shark
suddenly
the slip round to a bay
the beach within reach and you in the shallows
holding the sun.

The sex we have

The sex we have drags home half-ruined street furniture
to barricade the hallway against winter
it insists on standing too close at the bus stop
wearing a waterproof that smells of digestives
it hasn't learnt the subject from the object
protractors its name into the soft wood of the science table
roaches the report card
licks addresses off the envelopes
the sex we have falls in love with things singularly
eats them looking you dead in the eye
and regurgitates them onto the doorstep
the sex we have presses its face into your chest
heaves your ribs apart and head bangs until the jabbering quits
the sex we have untucks the sofa throw and scatters pillows
surges white goods
oops out the boiler light as we finish

Induction

They listen to my two heartbeats.
How is Mummy feeling.
A good birth happens when Mummy is relaxed.

I lie down, wired-up
to look at a framed picture
of a dog on a beach.

Here is a booklet about the amniotic sweep.
Here is a booklet on pain relief.
Here is a booklet on injections to hurry along placenta delivery.
Try eating some pineapple.
You have 24 hours before we insist.

Inside her heart thrums, she sings.
We look at trees losing leaves together,
we look at the distance of hills and spires.

When I'm sure the wind is blowing
so loud I can't even hear,
I say *come out and see.*

My mother's aria

My mother went into labour holding a sledge hammer
in a house with no floorboards or hot water.

My mother went to a hospital with black iron gates
6 weeks early in snow in December.
My dad took cheese sandwiches;
Wear your hair down he said.

I was backwards moving forwards
leaving my shoulder behind – my mother roared
while outside the snow got deep.

We are sorry for your loss, we will take care of your wife.
But my mother roared
and the doctor arrived from the Opera

wearing a cape to reach into my mother
and pull me out broken
to my mother's singing.

We will look after your wife, they told my dad,
as the doctor in his cape left to catch the last aria.

I love you so much that I want to explain

What a heart is other than a fact:
a radio fluting French disco
4 head boys holding doors
a traffic jam of atoms
a plug socket overcrammed
a sound system of lub-dub
troupes and troupes of acrobats
a home economics experiment
a stag on a racetrack
a lamp in park fog
a feeling freezer
a camera on long lens
a peeled fist.

Acknowledgements

Krystelle Bamford:
Earlier versions of these poems have appeared in *Under the Radar* ('Wake'), *Be the First to Like This: New Scottish Poetry* ('Two Lies: the deer') and *The Scotsman* ('Dad').

Claire Cox:
An earlier version of 'Funeral' appeared in *Ink, Sweat & Tears* and was Pick of the Month for February, 2019.

Hannah Jane Walker:
Poems have appeared in earlier versions with Nasty Little Press (Luke Wright and Sally Roe), in *Ink, Sweat and Tears,* and *Popshot* magazine. With many thanks to Caroline Bird and Joe Dunthorne for their advice and mentoring on earlier versions of these poems.